CW00642864

THE GAME OF LOVE AND D

JOHN HEATH-STUBBS

THE GAME OF LOVE AND DEATH

with drawings by Noel Connor

ENITHARMON PRESS 1990

First published in 1990
by the Enitharmon Press
40 Rushes Road
Petersfield
Hampshire GU32 3BW

Text © John Heath-Stubbs 1990
Illustrations © Noel Connor 1990

ISBN 1 870612 95 7 (paper)
ISBN 1 870612 01 9 (cloth)

The Enitharmon Press acknowledges
financial assistance from Southern Arts

Set in 10pt Ehrhardt by Bryan Williamson, Darwen
and printed by
Antony Rowe Limited, Chippenham, Wiltshire

ACKNOWLEDGEMENTS

Some of the poems have appeared in *The Tablet*, *The Financial Times*,
PN Review, *Agenda*, *Outposts*, *Prospice*, *The Anglo-Welsh Review*, *Critical
Survey*, *The Literary Diary (Waterstone) 1989*, *The Island of the Children*
(Fortune Books) and *Causley at Seventy* (Peterloo Poets).

CONTENTS

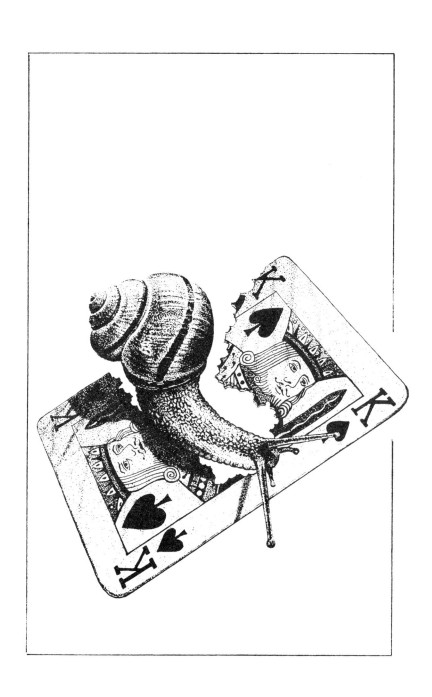

He cut. I shuffled. He began to deal.
"We'll play" said Death, "our green baize table
Be the four-cornered world. And we have partners –
This one is mine – he's dummy." "And I know him –
He's your twin brother and his name is Sleep."
"Some say they cannot tell us two apart;
And maybe that innocuous non-player
Is really Death, and I am nothing more
Than just a leering phantom in your dreams."
"And who" said I "is given me for partner?
This little yobbo, hauled in from his street game,
Improperly dressed in a pair of tattered pinions
And a quiver full of darts a tenuous G-string
Ties around his narrow downy loins?"

Death led the four of clubs, the Devil's four-poster;
But I had got the wish-card, nine of hearts.
And after that he played the Curse of Scotland.
I looked into my hand – it seemed a poor one:
The Kings were all the mean-faced Henry Tudor,
Grandson of devious Owen, and the Queens,
Desperately clutching at their fragile flowers,
Were all the sad Elizabeth of York.
The Jacks, in their flat caps of maintenance,
Were knaves, and unreliable. All of them feared
The King of Spades, his drawn and brandished sword.
And Death poured out a stream of spades – black Spanish blades,
Pointed inexorably against my breast.

As for my partner, what sort of game was his?
He spilled the heart's blood from our chalices.
He snapped our batons, and he squandered
All our small change of diamonds. Which was the Joker –
He or our opponent? I began to wonder.

Death laid another spade upon the table;
It was the nine, and followed by the ace.
Then all at once love played the ace of hearts,
And, "Hearts are trumps!" he shouted – "Always have been,
Ever since the founding of the world,
So you can grin on the other side of your face."
"The other side of my face," pale Death replied
"Perhaps is more like yours than men suppose."
He has the last word always, that one. So
The game went on, and it is still proceeding.

MIDWINTER

Midwinter robin wistfully sings:
Crickets chirp around the town incinerator.

From frozen tundra the wild geese,
And the wild swans, the whoopers, are come.

December's lumbering hearse
Brings up the rear of the months' procession.

With transparent fingers, blinded Lucy
Draws the curtains of the shortest day.

Under the hard soil, the shoots
Of snowdrop, aconite, crocus –

A time for taking stock,
For fresh beginnings.

MARY MAGDALEN, MARTHA
AND LAZARUS IN PROVENCE

A ship sailed into shore –
Martha and Lazarus it bore,
And Mary Magdalen.

Mary did penance in a cave,
Although she surely knew
That she had been forgiven,
And she would enter through the gates of heaven.

Martha converted the whole countryside.
She liked things tidy. She repressed
Tarasc, the horror,
Just like a cockroach in her Bethany kitchen.

But Mary in her damp and smelly cave,
Had learned to love the lively little roaches.

Their brother Lazarus was of the company,
And, having died already,
There was no message he could give
Excepting "Death is nothing that you need to fear".
To him it seemed so obvious
It almost became tedious,
And in the end he yawned, and went to sleep again.

At Barton-on-Sea, *ci-devant* Hampshire,
A block of flats collapses;
A man is trapped in the rubble. Well, well, well –
And this was the place I spent my earlier years in!
The first time, I'll be bound,
It's ever got in the news.

The pier at Shanklin, Isle of Wight,
Likewise is destroyed – its amusement arcade.
This I remember too. If you inserted a penny
The gates of a prison-model swung open
To reveal the condemned cell – the victim prepared,
While the little puppet chaplain, in his white surplice,
Bobbed up and down, desperately praying;
There were film shows you could also work –
Rin Tin Tin, the benevolent and enlightened
Alsatian dog; and What The Butler Saw –
Which was mostly underclothes; a self-operated
Violin, hardly Stradivarius,
Indulged in double stopping;
Electric shock machines
Would test, or maybe stimulate, your virility.
But all these, I guess,
Were long ago superseded, relegated
To the museum or the scrapyard.
In this digital age they must have been replaced
With more sophisticated gew gaws.

I am affronted by this hurricane.
It seems to have had a special animus
Against pleasure and culture. At Chichester Cathedral
Stained-glass windows are blown in;
The while in Prinny's stately pleasure dome
A pinnacle crashed into the music room.
A puritan wind, a roundhead wind, you'd say –
As if it contained the soul of Oliver Cromwell.
For that departed, as we know,
Into a great storm, in horror and anguish.
"Can a man fall from grace?" it howled, it muttered.

TO ONE GOING TO PARIS

So you're off to Paris, Adam? I would put
Paris into your hands, have her hold you
In her cupped hands – the feminine city,
With her river, gliding under her bridges,
And the accordion music
Blaring an embarkation for Cythera.

Vernal, autumnal, she is – or else, in winter,
Chilly and grudging in her draughty bars,
And in summer, as now,
Parched in her heat, or under
The girlish tears of her rain.

So you will find her, as each one finds her.
The same and different. The Paris I knew
Was of the later nineteen-forties,
War's aftermath, when we arrived
With twenty-five pounds in our pockets, to live
For a fortnight, perhaps, on omelettes,
Cheese and cheap wine, and now and then
Stuffed tomatoes at Raffi's. The left bank –
The bugs that pinched
In that small hotel on the Rue du Bac,
The stinking pissoirs – and the cafés:
Les Deux Magots for Sartre watchers;
On the opposite side of the boulevard the louche
Reine Blanche, with wall-to-wall
Mirrors (someone I know –
He had drunk too much, and his eyesight was bad –
Was the first person ever, since Narcissus,
To try and pick himself up)
And the Bar Vert in the Rue Jacob
Where, in a room upstairs, Edric Connor
Sang spirituals and ballads:
"Si le roi savait ça, Isabelle –
Isabelle, si le roi savait ça ..."

But there she will be for you, ancient and youthful,
Fickle and constant, wise and frivolous.
She is Saint Genevieve's city,
Resolute against Attila
And Villon's city against Burgundy,
Heroic city of barricades;
A thrifty housewife she is,
With a baton of bread and a bag of onions;
And a swallowtailed Sister of Saint Vincent de Paul;
An old cocotte in her beauty, which like all beauty
Beckons, and cheats, and fades.

FLOWERS, AND A WARNING

Push open the gate, and there they are –
The seasons jumble in a retrospective glance –
My first tentative crocus and aconite,
Self-regarding narcissus and the drunken tulip,
A few roses maybe, but not thornless,
Heavy, over-florid paeony-heads, and monstrous poppies
Beckoning to dream and to illusion,
Love-in-a-mist, and love-lies-bleeding,
Scruffy candytuft and saxifrage;
Likewise the prose of my vegetable-patch.

And now it's October there'll be chrysanthemums
With earwigs in them, there'll be Michaelmas-daisies.
Take them, such as they are, but do not dig too deep,
Dear, in the compost heap.

BC-AD

The *Pax Romana* – spurious:
A knock-out blow, delivered
By the most ruthless contender
Among a band of rival thugs.

The good roads are for the tax-gatherers;
The military discipline, the legions' tread,
For the extending boundaries.

Neck and foot the slaves are shackled.
In specious freedom, the barbarian,
Lousy, wrapped in a tattered hide,
Scuttles about the frontier,
Drinking kumiss from his grandfather's skull.

Famine and pestilence an ambient sea,
Too turbid for the halcyons' brooding.

In all this darkness, one small point of light – it shines
Out of a foul stable, between
A pair of commonplace quadrupeds.

It burns, now blue as the heavens of faith,
Now green as the hopeful shoots of spring,
Now fiery red like pain.

And from this seed expands
The lover's rose, the rose of revolution,
And shall continue to expand until
It touches the limits of eternity.

SEVENTEEN HUNDRED AND EIGHTY-NINE
(Bicentenary of Blake's *Songs of Innocence*)

The fortress fell – tyranny age-old,
Black ignorance, and cruelty, and injustice,
With the insolent levity that says to the starving
"Why can't you eat cake?"

That blissful morning of July, who might discern,
Beyond the bright, brave Phrygian cap,
A blood-stained blade descend –
Humane and rational machine of death?
The harlot of the abstract reason
Enthroned in the cathedral.
The lost traveller, the little boy lost,
Pursues a vapour still.

In Albion, in London's Golden Square
(Hovered above him quadrate golden Jerusalem),
A youthful craftsman, flaming-haired,
Corrodes with strong acid of revolution
The tablets of history, takes in hand
The honest tools of his trade, as he engraves
His songs and double images. He frames
The lamb in all its fearful symmetry,
Innocence of the tiger.

William Blake, towards Eternity
Ascending in Elijah's chariot – we know
The rose polluted by the secret worm,
Weariness of the sunflower;
And we have walked through every chartered street.

The vision of experience is ours.
You who guided Samuel Palmer's footsteps,
Where Virgil's shepherds pipe by Beulah's streams,
Show us once more the innocent vision: teach us
That, also, is valid.

Well then, two whole centuries have passed away
Since first that noble lord observed the light of day.
For us, perhaps, the comment has to be ironic –
Romantic modes are out, and specially the Byronic.
His tuppence-coloured heroes – those Corsairs and Giaours –
Hit the taste of his time, but hardly speak to ours.
Nowadays it's Don Juan seems to ring more bells:
"That doggerel satirist" (to quote H.G. Wells)
"With" – he said – "the philosophy of a man-about-town"
Is evidently the Byron who enjoys current renown.
That combination of wit, of feeling, and of rage
Is somehow in key with the spirit of our age.

He found his death, that which perhaps all along he
Most ardently desired from the start at Missalonghi.
He would go no more a-roving, being prepared to shed
His blood for Hellenic freedom. But what severed his thread
Was fever, cruel as passion. The Greek and wine-dark wave
Laments him still. Let myrtles deck his English grave.

THE THREE IDOLS

Each time we kiss, there are three great idols
That stand in the corners of the room.
Satan's chief agents in our time they are,
Just as in Blake's were Bacon, Newton and Locke.

"Genetic wastage!" says honest hardworking Darwin;
"Oedipus complex!" says courteous Viennese Freud;
"Bourgeois decadence!" says Karl Marx –
His sad whiskery puzzled face
With not a trace of anger in it.

In the fourth corner stands another –
His name is Orc or Eros, and
He has not spoken, not one single word.

VILLANELLE
On a theme from the Rubáiyát

"Alas, that spring should vanish with the rose,"
Sighed Omar – Ah how fragile all delight! –
"That youth's sweet-scented manuscript should close!"

But what if Time and Change be not our foes,
But strong, just angels? Then the phrase proves trite –
Alas, that spring should vanish with the rose!

Age can bring wisdom. Death may be – who knows? –
The gateway to Eternity. It's right
That youth's sweet-scented manuscript should close.

But there's not one, not one, as I suppose,
Who has not whispered in the chilly night
"Alas, that spring should vanish with the rose,
That youth's sweet-scented manuscript should close."

THE DWINDLING ONES
For Charles Causley

Upon your Cornish moors, I've read somewhere,
There dwells a race of beings para-human,
Who, for some ill they did, curse they incurred,
Are doomed continually to dwindle. Once they were giants,
Looming out of the mist, bawling into the storm-wind,
And then of super-human stature, great pine trunks their spears,
Hurling huge rocks for chuck-stones;
After, human sized, then more and more dwarfish –
Mannikins, midgets, elvish urchins,
Pixie-ish carousers out of acorn-cups,
Bee-sucking cowslip-lurkers like Ariel;
Then miniscule, like tiny bugs
(Their war with the pismires is an epic theme)
Or gossamer-drifting money-spiders,
Exiguous as fleas, as thrips, as cheese-mites;
And then dimension of the animalcula –
Horsed on the paramoecium, the rotifer a Charybdis,
Until at length they pass, with the viruses,
Through the fine filter of an eggshell-porcelain.

The end of the ages will be their vanishing-point:
At Gabriel's trump they'll disappear,
With an imperceptible puff, a supersonic twang.
They have all time, but no eternity.

But you and I, Charles, at three-score and ten,
Must learn we live on Chronos his overdraft.
We'll laugh and lie down, we'll go to bed with our boots on,
And thank God for His bounty of mortality.

HOMAGE TO ROBERT SCHUMANN
And in Memory of Kenneth Leisenring

"How can you enjoy" you said once, Ken,
"Robert Schumann, that incompetent composer,
Who never wrote a well constructed piece?"
I sighed and was silent, yet I should have spoken:
"Maybe you're right – is it the weak base line,
The muddy orchestration of his symphonies,
The melodies that drift, guided too much
By biedermeier sentiment and fantasy,
Reluctantly resolving in a lingering cadence?"

I should have said this, most of all have added:
"And yet I love him dearly."

Your vocation, Ken, was mathematics –
That discipline, that stripped beauty,
Had seized your mind, nurtured as it was
Upon mid-Western puritanism, perhaps was in your blood,
Part Scottish and part German. Music for you
Was Hindemith's dryness, Bach's complexity.

Oh Ken, it's now ten years have passed away,
Since you went to join the carnival –
Farewell to the heavy diabetic flesh, and hail
To possible, impossible resurrection. There,
Where souls like butterflies are flitting
Round the eternal harlequin, you're dancing now,
Now you are marching with the Davidsbündler.

31

The briefest statement can say all – each note
An incandescent spark, a point of light.
The tip of a cigar that glows
In nervous, trigger-happy GI night
Jerks a finger to release
The small, death-carrying bullet
That, whistling in the dark,
Seeks out, unerringly, its mark.

A VINEGAR-MOTHER

It floats, like a slice of discoloured liver,
Upon the surface of the stale wine,
Slowly converting it to vinegar.

Some people like to keep one as a pet,
In a crystal bowl, in dining room or parlour.
Each time they take their wine, they offer
A small libation to the vinegar-mother
To keep her strength up. I can see, of course,
This sharing of a pleasure has its point, especially
For those forlorn ones who must drink alone.
And yet I cannot quite suppose the creature
Is really cuddly, or affectionate.

Wingless and inert, the huge Dinornis
Said: "Why do they insist –
Those chaffinches and choughs and chickadees,
Starlings, storks and stock-doves, if you please –
On quite gratuitously cluttering
The skyways with their flitting and their fluttering?"
Replied the just as flightless Æpyornis:
"Surely they know
We gave all that up long ago."
Thus they opined, and blinked –
Two great struthious birds. But they became extinct –
Those others, for the present, still persist.

The rumour of whose beauty ran
Wildfire through Hellas, like the light that gathers
Round grey stocks of olives, trailing vines,
Or falls on sea waves, wine-dark under cliffs –

And now a bald hag, covered from head to foot
With scabs the itch-mite leaves, scratching, scratching,
Eternally scratching, but with no relief.

So, Dante saw her down in hell – and why?
Because she said, when a rich lover proffered her
A more than usually opulent gift for favours
She had rendered him, "Infinite thankyous!" –

The hell of the flatterers. But I would extend it
To a sickness of our time, which Dante
Hardly could have glimpsed, deflocculation of language.
We all know whom we'd shovel in that bolge –
Those who raped the word "fairy", those who clobbered "gay",
And those who've blurred and broken down
The line that runs between
"Disinterested" and "uninterested":
The disinterested shine for ever
Within the planetary heaven of Justice,
The uninterested bubble up,
With the slothful, through the mud.

Hardened offenders these – but I have lately noted
Those who say "refute", when all they mean
Is simply "contradict". It is not trivial –
Implying if you say a thing is not so
Long and loud enough you've proved your point.
This saps the body politic, this strikes at law –
Then there's the soft, insidious "if you like".
Otiose, it seems to sidle in
Whenever there's the slightest faint suspicion
Language may be becoming figurative.
How they fear metaphor and simile,
However worn. How much they must hate poetry –
A fortiori, if you like.

Aries, the constellated tup
(March's penfold, and his shepherd
The red-bearded Thracian war-lord)
Trotted along that starry track
We call the zodiac.

And it's there that he met up
With the great white bull, whom Venus
Leads with just a tenuous
Tether of spring flowers
Among her shimmering April bowers.

They ruminated, and concurred
On what presents were preferred
For you, since falls by chance
Your birthday near their boundary fence.

"I'll give the fanfare of my daffodils,
The spirit of my breezes blustering,
The thrush's courage, when he calls
Through treacherous weather, and his singing
Is a reiterated hope,
The sharpness of the tom-tit when he whets his saw."

"And I'll bring other guests – the cranky gowk,
The gentle whispering willow-wren;
And other blossoms – buttercup
In water-meadows with the lady's-smock,
The swallow's flower, the celandine,
On gravelled pathways harum-scarum
Dandelion, in hedgerows, green
With purple impudic pintle, wild arum."

THE ART OF LYING IN THE BATH
For John Fitton

I'm sorry for your indisposition, John,
Which was contracted, you said,
By lying too long in the bath.

Really accomplished bath-recumbents
Acquire the skill to turn on the hot tap
With their right foot, meanwhile
With the great toe of the left one, hauling up
The waste-plug – thus maintaining
An even temperature, a simmering heat.

Then they take down, from time to time,
From a specially designed shelf,
For their perusal, decidedly lengthy,
Rather tedious, and undeniably very great novels,
By Proust, by Tolstoy, or by Samuel Richardson.

This they diversify with operatic arias –
Composed by Cherubini, or Rossini,
Spontini, Meyerbeer, or even Wagner –
Not forgetting our own English or Irish Michael Balfe;
They dream they dwelt in marble halls, exult
In the heroic death of Nelson,
Excelsior-bannered they scale the Alpine heights,
Beseeching Maud to come into the garden,
On the banks of Allan Water, under the mistletoe bough.

That is the way it is done. I shan't aver it to be
Exactly my own practice.

THREE POEMS FOR CHILDREN

I wish I were a wood-louse,
In a green, mossy house,
Under a big flat stone:
  I would roll into a ball
  When people came to call,
And then they would leave me alone.

  To be a centipede
  Would be very nice indeed,
If I had fifty pairs of boots;
  Or an owl in a hollow tree,
  Singing "Nobody cares for me,
And I don't care two hoots".

  Bright Robin Redbreast
  In a kettle built his nest,
Beneath the wide, windy skies;
  What does he like to eat
  For his Christmas treat? –
Worm pudding, and squashed flies.

THE WITCH

Judy Cracko – she was a witch,
And lived in a muddy, smelly ditch:

But when the moon shone bright, she'd fly
On a tatty old broomstick, up in the sky,

With the bats, and the owls, and the booboo birds,
Shouting out loud the most horrible words,

Like Botheration, and Bottom, and Belly,
And Nurts and Nark it and Not on your Nelly!

Now the judge, Mr Justice Fuzzywig,
And the village policeman, Constable Pigg,

And Major Wilberforce Wotherspoon,
And a lady called Miss Prissy La Prune,

Put their heads together, and vowed
That sort of behaviour should not be allowed.

So they locked her up in a dungeon dim,
With her one-eyed pussycat, Smoky Jim.

But she didn't stay long in that prison cell –
She muttered a rather difficult spell:

Then seven red devils, with horns and tails,
And seldom manicured finger-nails,

And each with one great donkey's hoof,
Whirled Judy and Jim through a hole in the roof,

Over the seas and far away
To an island eastward of Cathay;
She's living there still, to this very day.

SAINT

There was a Cornish saint who dwelt
Beside the grey Atlantic wave;
And there, in a convenient cave,
By day and night, at prayer he knelt.
His food was seaweed, limpet-stew –
On feast days, half a mackerel too.
The tin miners and fisherfolk
Loved him. The gracious words he spoke
Brought them to share in his belief.
A credible report says he,
Wishing to voyage across the sea,
Would do so on an oak-tree leaf.
When he sang matins and evensong,
And lauds, and tierce and sext and nones,
The sea-birds gathered in a throng,
And all joined in with raucous tones –
The gannets, gulls, and terns, and lots
Of razorbills and guillemots;
A most delightful thing to hear
(Though they sang out of tune, I fear).

He lived till his hair was snowy white;
And passed away one shining night.
But then, descending, came a flight
Of angels through the starry skies:
Singing a strange and joyful psalm,
They dug his grave in the dawn-light calm;
While his soul rose to paradise.